Tarantula
Care

Quick & Easy Tarantula Care

Project Team
Editor: Brian Scott
Copy Editor: Phyllis DeGioia
Design: Patricia Escabi
Series Design: Mary Ann Kahn

T.F.H. Publications
President/CEO: Glen S. Axelrod
Executive Vice President: Mark E. Johnson
Publisher: Christopher T. Reggio
Production Manager: Kathy Bontz

T.F.H. Publications, Inc.
One TFH Plaza
Third and Union Avenues
Neptune City, NJ 07753

05 06 07 08 09 1 3 5 7 9 8 6 4 2

Library of Congress Cataloging-in-Publication Data
Breene, Robert G., III.
Quick & easy tarantula care / Robert Breene.
p. cm.
The biology of tarantula defined -- Housing -- Food and feeding -- Selected species of tarantula.
ISBN 0-7938-1031-0 (alk. paper)
1. Tarantulas as pets. I. Title: Quick and easy tarantula care. II. Title.
SF459.T37B74 2005
639'.7--dc22
2005026482

This book has been published with the intent to provide accurate and authoritative information in regard to the subject matter within. While every precaution has been taken in preparation of this book, the author and publisher expressly disclaim responsibility for any errors, omissions, or adverse effects arising from the use or application of the information contained herein. The techniques and suggestions are used at the reader's discretion and are not to be considered a substitute for veterinary care. If you suspect a medical problem, consult your veterinarian.

The Leader In Responsible Animal Care For Over 50 Years! ™
www.tfhpublications.com

Table
of Contents

Introduction to Tarantula's

So you're interested in tarantulas. Good for you! Buying this book before getting a tarantula is probably the best thing that you could do, but if you already have a tarantula and are looking to answer questions you have, then fear not as we will be covering many topics in a short space. Thankfully, most tarantulas are such tough little creatures that people often get away with many mistakes that would quickly kill other animals. In fact, you'll see the phrase "get away with" quite a few times in this book, especially since most tarantulas can survive the harsh conditions that their keepers unknowingly put them through, often for years. Generally, tarantulas are fun and easy to keep, especially if you know what not to do.

Buying A Tarantula

Many people buy their tarantulas from pet stores, although a large number of species can be safely ordered on the Internet, usually as spiderlings (baby spiders). If you are unfamiliar with tarantulas and don't know an experienced tarantula keeper, ask some questions before buying your tarantula.

- **How is it standing?**
  A tarantula with its legs tucked under it (classic spider death pose) that doesn't react, or reacts slowly to the touch, is likely sick or dying.

- **Does it have a water dish?**
  All tarantulas need water available if for no other reason than to replace fluids lost to an injury.

Tarantulas are generally tough and easy-to-care-for animals that do well in a wide range of environments. In fact, most tarantulas can survive in conditions that would normally kill other pets.

Don't forget to take into consideration the feelings that others may have about a large, hairy spider in their home, too.

- **Can the dealer tell you the scientific name of the spider?**
  As of press time for this book, there are 883 species of tarantulas known worldwide. All levels of the pet industry often make up common and scientific names unique to their own market. Knowing the scientific name of your spider is important for finding out what kind of care it needs. If the seller can't supply any information except a false common or scientific name, perhaps you should shop elsewhere.

- **Can the dealer tell you what sex it is or how old it is?**
  Mature males don't live very long, only a couple of months to two years or so depending on the species. Adult females may live for decades. All tarantulas with a legspan of two inches or more can be sexed by someone experienced with sexing (see Resources). If they can't tell you what sex an individual is, maybe you should look elsewhere.

Introduction to Tarantula's

Generally, captive bred tarantulas make better pets. In some cases, only captive-bred tarantulas are legal for sale or possession.

It would help tremendously if you knew whether the tarantula was wild caught or captive bred. Smaller tarantulas (half-inch to two-inch legspans) are probably captive bred. Captive bred tarantulas have less chance of having parasites or other maladies, but they may be inbred. Adult or large tarantulas sold in pet stores are usually wild caught. The problem is, nobody can tell you the age of a wild caught tarantula, and very often they can't tell you what species it is, either.

Tarantula Biology

T arantulas are spiders who belong to the kingdom Animalia in the phylum Arthropoda. They are further separated into the subphylum Chelicerata and are closely related to lobsters, crabs, and shrimps, as well as to insects, millipedes, centipedes, and several other creatures.

Spiders themselves can be further classified as members of the order Araneae in the class Arachnida, in addition to ten other orders including scorpions, harvestmen, whipscorpions, mites, and ticks, among others. Tarantulas specifically belong to the family Theraphosidae, one of 110 currently recognized spider families.

Tarantulas are unique creatures who inhabit some interesting habitats throughout their range. To do so, they must have specific anatomical features. One of these features is urticating hair on their bodies, sometimes also referred to as setae.

This Mexican redknee tarantula has released some of its urticating hairs. Note the bald spot on the abdomen.

Urticating Hair

About 95% of all tarantula species from the New World (Americas) are armed with one or more types of urticating (bristles) hairs that the tarantula can flick or rub off the abdomen when disturbed. Tarantula species from outside the new world do not have these hairs.

There are six different types of urticating hair, Type I through Type VI. Some are airborne, but others are not. Some people may develop allergies or sensitivity to the hair, while others are completely unaffected by it. The hair is thought to help keep small mammals or birds from eating the tarantula, but it may deter fly and wasp parasites, too.

This photo shows the eggs, post-embryos, and young spiders of a pink toe tarantula.

Arachnid Developmental Stages

Arachnid developmental terminology is widely misunderstood and misused. The fertilized spider egg is called the embryo. Eggs are laid on a thick layer of silk. As the eggs are laid, sperm is released from a storage organ within the female and the eggs are fertilized. More silk is deposited on top of the eggs. The female then fashions the whole mass into an eggsac ranging in size from a pea to a tennis ball, depending on the species. The egg hatches into the postembryo. Hobbyists often call this stage

First instars may vary in appearance depending on the species of tarantula concerned.

"eggs with legs," since it looks like someone glued a mite by the tail end onto a tarantula egg. The spider in this stage does not eat and is nonmobile.

The postembryo molts (the first true molt) in the eggsac, and becomes the 1st instar. The 1st instar can walk around but doesn't feed. While still within the eggsac, the 1st instar molts, becoming the 2nd instar. In the 2nd instar, the yolk in the egg supplied by the mother runs out at some point and the spiderling must begin to eat. The 2nd instar is also the stage the tiny tarantulas emerge from the eggsac. After the next molt, the animal enters 3rd instar, then the 4th and so on.

What's an Instar?

An instar is the term used when an insect is in between molts of their exoskeleton. Some specimens may molt as many as 20 or more times throughout their lives while others may only molt a few times. Those tarantulas that only molt a few times during their lives are usually males.

Once the spiderlings are fully motile, they are usually separated by the keeper and given their own enclosure to grow in.

The number of molts prior to sexual maturity is not constant in most, if any, tarantula species. Depending upon species and the sex of the individual, there may only be a small number of molts after the 2nd instar. The number of molts can be as little as three in the case of males of some species, or they may molt over 20 times (if appropriate, 19th instar is the name of an individual molting that many times).

Instar numbers stop when the spiderling reaches the antepenultimate instar, which is the instar preceding the penultimate instar. The penultimate instar is the stage immediately prior to sexual maturity. After molting into a sexually mature individual capable of reproduction, the spider is called an adult, or the ultimate instar. Males are not likely to survive the ultimate instar for long except in captivity. Tarantula females keep on going past ultimate instar, and continue into postultimate instars. The first molt of an ultimate instar female is called the 1st postultimate instar, then the 2nd postultimate instar, and so on.

Many terms are used inappropriately by hobbyists. Spiderling is a term so entrenched it may never go away and we will continue to use it here. People frequently refer to the 1st through 3rd or 4th (or more) instars as spiderlings. Subadult is a term used widely by enthusiasts to indicate a large immature spider nearing the ultimate instar, but many new to the hobby don't know this. Juvenile is another term used. It supplies no information except the tarantula is not an adult.

Quick & Easy Tarantula Care

Anatomy and Internal Organs

The outer layer of a tarantula is called the exoskeleton. It's made up of the cuticle and epidermis. Tissues, muscles, and organ systems are suspended inside the internal cavity of the exoskeleton.

The cuticle is made up of 40 to 60% chitin (complex sugars) and protein of each compound either way. Sections of the chitin are greatly strengthened by a hardening process called tanning or sclerotisation. This hardened portion is

A tarantula's head is fused to its thorax.

called the exocuticle. The cuticle is not very water resistant. It's made waterproof by waxes, which are secreted through pore canals that carry the waxes to the outside of the tarantula, partially making up thin outermost cuticle layers called the epicuticle.

The spider head is fused to the thorax and covered on top by a shield called the carapace. Together, they are called the prosoma or cephalothorax. The chelicerae are the foremost set of appendages

Regeneration

Spiders have the ability to regenerate lost chelicerae, along with the pedipalps, legs, and spinnerets.

All About Legs

Tarantulas have eight legs, and each leg has seven segments. From the body outward, the leg segments include the coxa, trochanter, femur, patella, tibia, and tarsus.

and include the fangs. The fangs are used to inject venom, paralyzing the prey and possibly aiding digestion somewhat. The chelicerae are also used to manipulate prey, tearing it apart and mixing it into a bolus mass for feeding.

In female and immature tarantulas, the next pair of appendages, called the pedipalps, appears as a small pair of walking legs with one segment (the metatarsus) missing. In males, the pedipalps are swollen and serve as secondary sexual organs or copulatory devices.

Sperm is stored in the male pedipalps and transferred to the female during mating. Most males (not all) also have a hook-like appendage on the underside of the tibia of the first pair of legs. They are used to hold the female upright by the fangs while mating. Female and immature spiders use the pedipalps largely as sensory devices and to manipulate prey.

Tarantulas have thick tufts of hair or setae on the tarsi that are called scopulae. The scopulae enable them to walk on smooth surfaces like vertical glass. They

Scopulae are setae found on the pads of the feet (tarsus) and are used to climb smooth surfaces—like glass!

don't function as suction cups. The force is simple physical adhesion aided by capillary action brought about by a thin film of water found on all surfaces.

Spider legs function in an interesting manner using muscles that bend the joints (flexors) or extend them (extensors). Two major leg joints between the femur-patella and the tibia-metatarsus are not equipped with extensor muscles. Instead, internal blood pressure is used to extend those segments.

The central nervous system is large and compact, basically forming one large ganglion. The brain is a large part of this ganglion. The ganglion is formed in the spider embryo when all the abdominal ganglia migrate forward and fuse with the cephalothorax appendage ganglia, forming a brain that is huge compared to the body size.

The basic units of the digestive system consist of the foregut, midgut, and hindgut. Spiders predigest food externally, taking in only liquefied material with particles not much larger than a

This male Mombassa golden starburst tarantula shows the usual group of eyes at the front of the carapace.

single micron in size. Tarantula venom serves primarily only to paralyze, kill, or at least slow down the movements of the prey. Recently, scientists found different digestive enzymes in the venom, so in some species venom may do more than aid in prey capture. Digestive enzymes are regurgitated onto or into the prey from the mouth. The liquefied food is filtered through mouth structures and taken in through the sucking stomach, a powerful pump located in the cephalothorax.

The foregut in spiders is subdivided into the mouth, pharynx, esophagus, and sucking stomach. The spider midgut begins behind the sucking stomach still within the cephalothorax. Tubes, called the gastric caeca, branch off the midgut and serve as pouches for food storage. The pouches may be extremely extensive, some even extending into the cephalothorax and legs. Within the abdomen, the gastric caeca can also become extensive, penetrating a large part of the abdomen. The large food storage pouches are one of the reasons many tarantulas can go months or even years without food.

The Malpighian tubules, which are similar in function to vertebrate kidneys, empty into the midgut near its end. The

The foregut begins with the mouth, which is also where the chelicerae (fangs) are found.

Quick & Easy Tarantula Care

Tarantula Blood

The blood is usually clear, blue-tinted, or a cloudy gray because the blood cell that carries oxygen and carbon dioxide contains copper, not iron as with back-boned animals.

hindgut in spiders consists of a short tube connecting the midgut to the anus.

The spider heart lies near the top of the abdomen where it pushes blood forward toward the head. The arterial system is developed in many spiders. The aorta branches extensively into arteries leading throughout the cephalothorax. The arteries may reach as far as the spider's feet. After leaving the arteries, the blood passes into the open body cavity and washes over the organs delivering oxygen and picking up carbon dioxide before heading back to the heart by way of the booklungs. Tarantulas don't have veins directing the blood back to the heart as mammals and other vertebrates do.

Tarantulas use two pairs of booklungs for gas exchange. Booklungs have an extremely thin series of plates, stacked on top of each other, kept separated by a field of struts. Blood flows between the plates and gas exchange takes place with the air between them. Blood returning from the cephalothorax is shunted through the booklungs, becoming oxygenated before returning to the heart. The reproductive system and spinnerets with associated silk glands are also contained within the abdomen.

Molting

Molting is one of the most perilous times for tarantulas. They are nearly defenseless while the process is taking place. A large percentage of deaths of captive tarantulas occur during molting.

This beautiful little tarantula lies next to its freshly shed exoskeleton. Note the greatly increased size of the spider.

During molting, all old exocuticle and epicuticle is shed, including parts of the fore and hindgut. The endocuticle is dissolved by molting fluid. During this time, procuticle is secreted under the old endocuticle to later become the new cuticle.

Molting Problems

A tarantula that is upside-down with its legs in the air, or on its side, is almost certainly molting. Don't try to turn it over or touch it, or you may injure it. The exception to this is if it begins molting while upright. With larger individuals, you may have to gently help the molting tarantula turn over onto its side to prevent leg damage or loss. Small tarantulas (one-inch legspan or less) can often get away with molting upright.

After molting, several days to weeks may be needed for the exoskeleton to harden and begin feeding. Don't feed the tarantula until it recovers and begins acting "normal" again. This may be as little as 2 or 3 days for young spiderlings and as long as 2 or 3 weeks for older tarantulas.

Quick & Easy Tarantula Care

Six Steps to a Successful Molt

1. Tarantula preparing to molt.

2. Splitting open the carapace.

3. Extraction of legs, fangs, and foregut.

4. Discarding the abdomen.

5. After the molt, the spider will remain motionless during recovery.

6. The tarantula is on the right, shed skin is on the left. Note the regenerated leg.

Healthy adult tarantulas will usually complete a molt well before 48 hours. Rarely will a specimen survive if the molt lasts longer but don't give up hope, some will make it through.

There are warning signs telling you a molt is imminent. The most common one is they stop feeding, sometimes for weeks or months prior to a molt. A second warning is the construction of a molting mat. This is a thin layer of silk tarantulas use to lie upon as they molt. The best indicator of an impending molt for most new world tarantulas is the darkening of the abdomen to a purple-black hue. The best place to look for this is on the abdomen under bright light.

Adult tarantulas usually complete a molt within hours. If your spider gets stuck in its molt, you may need to help it out. Try wetting it with water or water with glycerin diluted 1 part to 20 parts, but don't get any near the booklung openings. If molting lasts over a day or so, drastic measures may be needed. You can use a pair of forceps and gently try to pull off the old exoskeleton by pulling on the ends of the old leg skin. Few tarantulas survive a molt if it takes over 48 hours, but some have, so don't give up all hope.

Handling For Examination

A little should be said about how tarantulas can be handled before delving into trauma and disease diagnoses and treatment. Tarantulas

Quick & Easy Tarantula Care

who are used to being handled by their keepers can be easily examined and treated as needed. Handling tarantulas that show a high degree of defensive behavior can be a big problem. If the handler is anxious about picking up the tarantula, the end result is often a dropped animal who is then injured worse than it previously was.

Handling can be accomplished in several ways. The most common is coaxing it onto the hand from the side or floor of the cage. A more defensive tarantula can be guided into a glass jar or clear plastic bag for examination. For more de-fensive individuals, the tarantula can be slowed down by placing them, cage and all, into a refrigerator for 5 to 20 minutes or so (not the freezer!)

There are trends within certain genera or species tending to be more laid back, or alternately more reactive, but there are always excep- tions with individuals. Some Chilean rose tarantulas are highly defensive; a species thought to be quite mild mannered. Others, like cobalt blue tarantulas, a species that supposedly bites rapidly with little or no provocation, can have individuals that act like little harmless kittens.

Note: If you have any doubts about your ability to pick up a large spider without dropping it, don't try. Even short falls may hurt or kill your spider.

The author handling a stunning example of an Indian ornamental tarantula (Poecilotheria regalis).

The fact is that all tarantulas can be handled if the handler knows what to do. If you can read the spider's body language, know how to calm even the most spirited individuals by gently stroking them with a soft camel hair brush, and take enough time, nothing is impossible with tarantulas. There are few people who know how to do this, and the methods can't adequately be taught, only gained through experience. Confidence without apprehension is one of the keys.

The only advice I can offer on handling is if you are nervous about it, don't do it. If you're jumpy, the chances are greater for an accident that often ends up hurting or killing the tarantula. If you're not entirely comfortable with the idea of handling a tarantula, don't put yourself through it. Some species do have venom that can, in some instances, make bites extremely painful and cause other alarming temporary neurological symptoms, such as cramping and numbness.

Fungal, Bacterial, and Blister Problems

Most of these kinds of problems are either directly caused or aggravated by the environmental conditions in the cage or room in which the tarantula is kept. Problems with fungal growth, both on the animal and in the cage, are not uncommon.

Using Pillbugs and Sowbugs

Terrestrial isopods (pillbugs and sowbugs) are easy for nearly everyone to find and use. Pillbugs and sowbugs (sometimes collectively called woodlice outside the United States) are land crustaceans. They eat decaying organic material, such as prey remains, and fungi. The addition of a few pillbugs or sowbugs from time to time may help reduce or eliminate these substances. The isopods may also help free cages of mites by consuming the resources the mites would otherwise use to increase their numbers. Pillbugs and sowbugs can be found under vegetation around the edges of homes and in gardens.

Fungal Growth

If the fungal growth is on the animal, certain fungicides at very low concentrations have been used with some success. A dilute solution of the fungicide Benomyl, baking soda, or gentian violet applied with a soft brush has been used with success for fungus growing on exoskeletons. As for mold, using a high efficiency particulate air (HEPA) filter or a negative ion generator may cut down on mold and other problems in specific arthropod rooms. They may also be useful to control loose urticating hair in the room.

Bacterial Infections

Bacterial infections are a mystery. Some may be characterized by discharges from the mouth, anus, booklung, or genital openings. Irrigation of the affected regions with a solution of 50 mg tetracycline to 25 ml fluid (saline or water) has worked on some infections.

Bacterial and fungal infections are very harmful to the tarantula. Sadly, the area of arachnid medicine is still in its infancy.

One possible bacterial infection is often seen in North American *Aphonopelma* species. A white, hardened crusty substance covers the anus and surrounding area of affected individuals. It appears to plug up the tarantula, preventing normal excretion of wastes. The excrement of tarantulas is most often white; the solidified patch doesn't appear to be simply dried excrement, but it might be. The only treatment known is dabbing the area with glycerin or some other softening agent using a cotton swab. Regardless of treatment, tarantulas afflicted with the condition die within a few months after it is first noticed.

Blistering

In some tarantula species, especially in heavy-bodied tarantulas, a blister appears on the underside of the abdomen, sometimes on the other sides. If the spider is immature, the blister grows as the tarantula molts. It appears as a slightly raised lump lighter in color than the surrounding exoskeleton. It may be caused or aggravated by coarse or rough substrate such as aquarium gravel. The blisters are also suspected of being caused by a fungus or bacteria.

Most individuals afflicted with the blister eventually die when the lesion ruptures. However, in some instances, the lesion may disappear after a molt. The tarantula may live for years before the lesion ruptures (usually during molting), killing the spider. Treatment entails switching to a less irritating substrate, such as vermiculite, potting soil, or top soil. Dabbing the blister with glycerin, tetracycline, or fungal medication with a cotton swab may or may not help.

Ants, Mites, and Other Pest Problems
Tarantulas can suffer from a rather wide assortment of parasitic /predatory problems. The aggressors in these cases may be anything from the tiniest of mites to large and aggressive ants.

Ants
Ants can present a tremendous problem, and have been known to injure or kill tarantulas. The problem species are few, and include primarily fire ants, the Argentine ant, and the pharaoh ant, although a few others may sometimes pose a problem.

Baits and barriers are the key to control. What works for one person may not work for the next. For fire ants, and possibly the Argentine ant, find the colony and treat it with Amdro™ according to label instructions. For pharaoh ants, try the various ant baits sold in hardware stores. Powdered cinnamon has been known to repel them.

Barriers can be effective. Preventive sticky tapes, or material such as Tanglefoot™, can be used to barricade ant entrances into arthropod cages. Placing the cage on pylons set into a pan of soapy water can work. The best advice is to be as persistent in attacking the ants as they will be on your arthropods.

Mites

Mites are probably the most commonly encountered problem when keeping arthropods in captivity. As with humpbacked flies, they are probably there living off prey remains. If mite populations build to high levels, they may invade the moist surfaces of the booklungs in tarantulas to the point of suffocating them.

Several options are available for controlling mites. The tarantula can be removed and the cage thoroughly cleaned with dishwashing soap, preferably outdoors. Make sure all the mites are removed from the contaminated cage and start over with mite-free substrate.

As for the tarantula itself, never use soaps or alcohols to attempt to remove the mites from them. These are lethal substances to tarantulas. A water bath with no soap has been known to work in clearing mites from scorpions and spiders, although you are bound to miss some, and they will likely be back.

Acaricides of various brands are too risky, since often a material that will kill the mites is likely to also kill the tarantula. Diatomaceous earth, used for many reptiles, may also harm the tarantula within the cage, not just the mites. Two spotted spider mites appear to be the species implicated in most harmful infestations. Many other mites don't seem to bother the tarantulas, and remain at low numbers within the cage.

All species of tarantulas are subject to mites. Always be sure that the cage substrate is clean and mite-free.

Tarantula Biology

A biological control alternative has been used for many years. Predator mites prey on the mites that can harm the tarantulas. These are sold by many biological control agent supply companies. Few if any problems have been reported between the predator mites and tarantulas.

The predator mite is available from companies listed in the Resources section at the end of this book. Half a tablespoon full of the vermiculite in which the mites are shipped per cage or less will probably be enough for mite control.

Humpbacked Flies

Many areas around the world sometimes have severe problems with humpbacked flies, family Phoridae (although there are others). The flies probably don't normally kill captive arthropods, but can be a persistent and nearly always present nuisance.

In the United States, the most common species is a small gray-colored fly. The females of this fruit fly-sized fly lay their eggs on discarded prey remains or on other suitable available organic material, such as bodies of uneaten prey dying in the cage before they were consumed. Under certain conditions, the larvae may attack the tarantula's booklungs seeking moisture to the point of suffocating it and feeding upon the remains.

A fly larva can be seen on the back of this tarantula.

Sanitation, moisture reduction, and barriers are the methods used to control humpbacked flies. Remove prey remains and uneaten prey bodies frequently. A microscreen small enough to prevent the tiny adult flies from getting in the cages should be fitted on all ventilation

Quick & Easy Tarantula Care

openings, no matter how small. Introducing small species of common cobweb weavers found inside buildings in your area into large tarantula cages may help in control, as long as they are not large or strong enough to eat your tarantula.

These flies often breed in well-watered indoor plants. Adding an inch or so of sand on the top of the soil in your indoor plants can reduce the problem, since they don't recognize sand as a place to lay eggs to produce more flies. Sticky flypaper strips may also aid in effective fly control.

Nematodes
Some species Nematodes (roundworms) may cause problems. There is no known remedy for an infected tarantula. Symptoms include a white liquid mass appearing on the mouth. You can attempt to wash the mass off, but few tarantulas survive a nematode infestation.

Trauma Treatment
Until recently, most serious injuries resulted in the death of the tarantula. Many are now being saved due to the development of new emergency treatments.

Cephalothorax/Abdomen Treatment
Wounds on the cephalothorax and abdomen are far more serious than leg wounds. Cephalothorax wounds are rare, but do happen and usually occur on the carapace. Abdominal ruptures are much more common, and can cause death within minutes if severe enough. The wound, whether on the abdomen or cephalothorax, requires rapid sealing. The ideal choice to seal the wound is the surgical tissue adhesive that veterinarians use (liquid stitches). Surgicel is probably perfect for the job, but a certified physician or veterinarian needs to dispense it.

Since the adhesive is not generally available to most people, some brand of super glue (cyanoacrylate glue) is the next best choice. Apply the glue directly on the wound. If the bleeding still hasn't stopped, place a small

Tarantulas that are kept in naturalistic vivariums are more likely to suffer from injuries compared to spiders that are kept in more simplistic setups. Always be prepared.

patch of paper towel or other tissue over the wound and re-apply the super glue. After the bleeding has stopped, two or three coats of artificial skin or nail hardener found in many stores or can be applied. Another possible material is Skin Patch™ or a similar product. These products are used by bowlers to seal missing skin quickly. Be sure to keep all these materials well away from the booklungs, mouth, and anus.

The treated wound will appear messy. All the treatment needs to do is stop bleeding and then you hope the spider begins internal repairs. The treatment materials will be shed upon the next molt, providing the spider survives the molt.

If the bleeding stops and the spider survives the treatment, supply it with plenty of water in an open dish so it can recover lost fluids. Currently, nothing further can be done.

Leg/Pedipalp Treatment
Past treatments for leg bleeding included materials like talc, cornstarch, and similar compounds intended to initiate clotting. Unless the wound was slight, the treatments didn't work more often than not. Super glue is still used by some, but it can be messy and difficult to use on legs, since the legs can become attached to each other or to the body creating further problems.

Triple nail hardener, nail mender, or any of the nail hardeners work well. The products are universally available, are easy to store, and are

Quick & Easy Tarantula Care

apparently harmless to larger tarantulas. It is still not recommended for smaller tarantulas with a legspan of under two inches. There is a second method described below for small spiders that is far better than nail hardener.

The legs of nearly all spiders are long and delicate. However, they are generally powerful and provide the spider with amazing speed when needed.

Almost all the ingredients of nail hardener can be extremely lethal to tarantulas. Logically, a chemically defenseless tarantula should quickly die if exposed to these formidable compounds, but they don't. Perhaps most toxic materials evaporate away too quickly to enter the tarantula's body and cause injury. Simply coat the wound, wait until it dries, then put on one or two more coats. If the leg is not too badly injured, the coating will be removed with the shed exocuticle during the next molt.

If the leg is broken or twisted, or the injury is a sizeable one, the following treatment should be used instead. If it isn't, the leg will likely be lost anyway during the next molt, and the tarantula may not start regenerating a new one in time.

Brand New Body Parts!

The legs and pedipalps are not the only items of spider anatomy that can regenerate. The chelicerae (including the fangs), labium, endites, and spinnerets are all capable of growing back. In one experiment, all eight legs of a spider were pulled off and the spider was hand fed until its next molt, when all legs reappeared, although smaller than the original legs. Two or three molts may be required for the legs to get back to normal size.

Tarantula Biology

Autotomy

Tarantulas can be induced to practice autotomy on a leg or pedipalp (voluntarily tossing it off), but a specific leg segment, the femur, should be grasped and not any other segment on the leg. If other segments are grasped, the spider may not give up the limb. Research done decades ago discovered that autotomy was a voluntary act on the part of the individual, since anesthetized spiders couldn't autotomize their legs.

A spider's leg is composed of seven distinct segments. Joined to the cephalothorax, the first leg segment is the coxa, followed by the trochanter. Both are thick, shortened segments. The trochanter is attached to an elongated femur. Autotomized legs always separate at the same joint, between the coxa and the trochanter. Once the femur is gripped with forceps, you may not have to pull to get the leg off. The spider may snap the coxa upwards while the femur maintains its position, acting as a brace.

Some individuals don't want to give up a leg or pedipalp. In this case, the femur must be grasped firmly with the forceps, and you must rapidly snap the femur up to get the spider to release the leg. It may take many tries and sounds awful, but it doesn't hurt the spider. When a badly bleeding leg comes off, the condition of the spider goes from critical to "all is well" instantly. Occasionally, the wound may later reopen. To prevent this, and to give you some insurance, triple coat the stump with nail hardener.

Quick & Easy Tarantula Care

Housing Your Tarantula

Housing for tarantulas falls into two distinct categories requiring different environmental conditions. Spiderlings compose one category, while larger immatures and adults make up the second. We'll start with larger immatures and adults.

Tarantulas can be divided into at least three groups according to the habitat to which they are adapted. The first is arboreal (living in trees or shrubs). The second and third tarantula types are burrowing species (dwelling in the soil or under rocks or roots). The two types of burrowing species are further separated into the obligate burrowers that are thought to require burrows, and opportunistic burrowers that take over and modify the burrows of other animals, and/or take advantage of crevices in rocky areas or around trees and shrubs. Some opportunistic species may wander along the ground at night and seek a different secluded sheltering spot each day, and may not have a permanent burrow.

Arboreal Tarantulas

Most arboreal species often create dense webbing within their cages. Some opportunistic burrowers also web up the cage profusely, so it isn't exclusive to arboreal species. Some, perhaps most, arboreal species are social to some degree. In nature, they tolerate and sometimes seek out the company of other individuals of the same species. Although it's tempting for hobbyists to keep arboreal species together in a colony, many spiders have been lost this way. A species known for social behavior can suddenly attack and kill others in captivity for unknown reasons, especially when the victim is molting.

Cage height is the main difference between the way arboreal and burrowing species are housed. Arboreal species can be housed in

shoe, sweater, or Tupperware™ boxes; Pet Pals (plastic cages sold in pet stores); aquariums of any size; or a specially-built cage 10 feet or more in height. These species are adapted to grip securely what they climb. There is some evidence that a few species may be capable of leaping from trees and gliding to escape predators.

Arboreal tarantulas can safely be placed in high enclosures.

Many arboreal keepers use pieces of cork bark or parts of tree branches or trunks for them to climb and make their silken retreats upon. Substrate is optional for arboreal tarantulas. Vermiculite is one old favorite substrate, as is soil, peat, or potting soil.

Many people have thought that several arboreal species need excellent ventilation. Whether this is critical has not been demonstrated, but good ventilation is never a bad idea for most tarantulas. Arboreal species appear to be less tolerant of moist, poorly ventilated cages than some of the larger burrowing tarantulas.

Good ventilation is not a bad idea in a setup for arboreal tarantulas.

Burrowing Tarantulas

As mentioned previously, there are two types of burrowing tarantulas. The first are the obligate burrows and the second are the opportunistic burrowers.

Obligate Burrowers

Obligate burrowers supposedly rarely modify preexisting structures, at least in nature, and excavate their own burrows themselves according to their habitat-specific needs.

Several inches of substrate may allow them to burrow, but in this situation you may only see your tarantula on rare occasions. Some keepers make artificial burrows where the inside of the burrow is visible through the side of the cage. This open side may be covered with a piece of cardboard when you are not viewing it to discourage the tarantula from webbing over the "window."

Housing Your Tarantula

Opportunistic burrowing species will take advantage of existing holes, crevices, and burrows.

Opportunistic Burrowers

Opportunistic burrowers may take advantage of existing habitats, modifying them for their needs. These habitats include fallen trees, under rocks, firewood stacks, rodent burrows, or crevices in the ground. Many individuals modify preexisting habitats for their own purposes, and much energy is saved doing this.

Burrowing tarantulas are not adapted to falling as are arboreal tarantulas, and the burrowing tarantulas can be easily injured or killed by a short drop measured in inches. Falling from the top of a too-tall cage is one of the most common ways burrowing tarantulas die in captivity. A common guideline is to be sure not to make the distance between the substrate and the cage top much higher than the outstretched legspan of the tarantula.

It's also important to keep sharp objects out of all burrowing species cages. The tarantulas may become injured falling against plants such as cactus with spines, other plants with sharp parts, rocks with sharp edges, and anything similar.

Pet Pals, sold in pet shops, work well for many species. Many plastic and glass containers can be adapted for tarantula homes. Make sure the tarantula cannot escape from whatever cage you use.

Cage Tops

If you use standard window screen-size mesh for cage tops, tarantulas may trap the claws at the ends of their legs in the mesh and lose or injure legs. Microscreen or hardware cloth is better than screen-size mesh.

Container Size

Containers should be no smaller than about two and a half times the legspan of the individual by one and a half times the legspan. Otherwise, the ground surface area size of the cage is up to you. People who own large numbers of tarantulas often choose small cages due to space limitations.

Humidity

Stagnant containers with high humidity can easily breed mold, fungi, bacteria,

Small plastic cages serve as perfect enclosures for many species of tarantulas—especially young spiders.

A tarantula in a moss-filled cage looks pretty but the humidity causes problems with mold and bacterial growth. Generally, drier is better.

mites, and other maladies. If your tarantula doesn't require high humidity, a water dish the size of a Petri dish, without a sponge, is sufficient. Place small, smooth stones in it to help prevent crickets from drowning. The water dish is satisfactory for humidity, even without taking any other moisture-increasing actions, especially misting. Misting accomplishes little except to irritate the tarantula. Certain species may, at least initially, require higher humidity, so finding out what species you have can be critical.

If there is one rule of thumb in keeping tarantulas, it is to keep the cage as dry as possible. The dryness will prevent most or all negative environmental conditions that may cause infestations such as mites, nematodes, fungi, and a host of other problems.

Some tarantulas are thought to require high moisture levels. I know of no species of tarantula that cannot be adapted to even the driest conditions, although it may take some time. Even species kept in what amounts to mud can be gradually adapted.

If the tarantula is not happy with conditions it feels are too dry, it will hang over its water dish for extended periods of time. If this happens, you can increase humidity by restricting ventilation using plastic wrap to cover 90% or so of the top, and keeping the water dish full. If this is not enough, and the tarantula still won't leave the water dish, try wetting the substrate with water in certain parts, but not all over.

Spiderlings

In the case of spiderlings, maintaining higher humidity is practiced by nearly all successful keepers. Tiny spiderlings can be kept in one-ounce deli cups with the tops perforated with pinholes; include a small amount of potting soil or vermiculite on the bottom of the cup. Many keepers also introduce a little sphagnum moss in which the spiderling may form its retreat. Misting is appropriate in this case. A short burst from a spray bottle on the side of the deli cup supplies the spiderling with water (it can drink the water droplets) and keeps the humidity within the small container elevated.

As the spiderling gets bigger, simply move it to a larger deli cup and use the same methods. Deli cups are inexpensive and can be purchased at your local restaurant supply store. Placing a half-inch or less legspan spiderling in a large 10 or 20-gallon aquarium can be dicey, since you may never be able to find it to feed it.

Cage Temperatures

For most tarantulas, the temperatures are best in the range between 70° and 89°F (21° and 31°C). The temperature at which each tarantula is maintained is largely a function of what the keeper has in mind for that spider. Spiders are poikilothermous (cold-blooded) and the ambient temperatures directly affect the rate of metabolism. The cooler the temperatures are, the slower the metabolism. The same is true when temperatures reach the upper 90s Fahrenheit, at which point metabolism begins to decrease from heat stress. If you have a female you are not going to breed, there's no reason to keep her in temperatures above 75°F (24°C). On the other hand, if you have an immature specimen that you want to reach adulthood quickly, the high 80s or even low 90s Fahrenheit would speed up the metabolism, causing the animal to feed more, molt, and grow faster; however, you need to check water and humidity conditions every few days or daily.

It's quite simple really, and the time it takes for development from egg or spiderling to adult depends on temperature and food. Years - sometimes as many as five or more depending on the species—can be shaved off the time it takes to reach maturity if kept at high temperatures with plentiful, nutritious food. Days or weeks can be cut off development times of

Glass cages that open from the front are popular enclosures for tarantulas.

immature specimens in eggsacs by increasing temperatures. However, the warmer the animals are kept, the faster the evaporation rates are, and desiccation problems can arise, especially for young immature spiders and spiderlings still within the eggsac. The warmer the cages are kept, the more frequently they should be checked for adequate moisture levels. Eggsacs taken away from the mother should be turned at least once a day.

Many tarantulas can probably be safely kept well below 75°F (24°C), at least for periods of time during the winter. With lower temperatures, problems with prey digestion and other problems occur more frequently, so feeding is not advised during these periods.

Food and Feeding

Carbohydrates, proteins, and vitamins are required by tarantulas for successful development. Certain fatty acids may or may not be required, but these fatty acids, in addition to the above, are usually found in sufficient amounts in the animal tissues tarantulas eat. Large amounts of protein are needed for egg production. Since tarantulas are predators and scavengers of other animals and are considered to be a high quality food, everything they need is in their prey.

Spider nutritional requirements are probably similar to those of predacious insects, but little research has been completed on the subject. One study suggested that three species of wolf spiders in the

field tended to prey upon a mixture of species that optimized the proportions of essential amino acids in their diet. Other studies also demonstrated that some wolf spiders benefit from a varied diet. Whether or not this is true for tarantulas remains uncertain, but varying the diet at least occasionally is a good idea.

Food Items

Tarantulas will feed on a variety of insects and other animals during all stages of their life. However, only a small number of these organisms are available to the common hobbyist. Recently, some on-line retailers have begun to offer a variety of potential prey animals that you can purchase as food for your spider.

Crickets

Crickets are the most common item fed to tarantulas owing to the relative ease of handling them, their availability locally or by mail

order, and the usual lack of problems encountered when feeding them to tarantulas. Many different cricket species can be used. The problem with crickets is that they are capable of harming or killing tarantulas under certain conditions, such as when a tarantula is

Crickets are widely available from many sources.

lethargic or ill, or when the tarantula is helpless during a molt. If your tarantula shows no interest in feeding on crickets after a few hours, or at most 48 hours, remove the crickets from the cage. Damp spots on the substrate can induce female crickets to lay eggs. Molting tarantulas have been injured or killed by starving newly-hatched pinhead crickets desperately seeking a meal.

Cockroaches

Cockroaches are frequently used to feed captive arthropods. Hissing cockroaches and other species are easily bred in captivity. The young nymphs of these cockroaches can come in handy as food items for smaller-sized tarantulas.

Reptiles and Amphibians

Reptiles and amphibians are sometimes used as prey items for tarantulas. Small frogs and toads have been used as tarantula food with no ill effects. A major prey source of certain ground dwelling tropical tarantula species in South America may be the specific frogs and toads found in high numbers on the forest floor. Skinks, anoles, other lizards, and even small snakes have been fed to captive arthropods without problems.

Beetles

Most beetles make excellent prey for tarantulas, especially June beetles; those are found in large numbers around outdoor lights during the

Grasshoppers and Katydids

Grasshoppers and katydids are suitable prey. Some people remove the back legs to make them easier to catch and to lessen the possibility of an injuring kick. Occasionally a tarantula will take raw hamburger tied to a string and brought abruptly to their attention. Other types of prey include moth and butterfly adults. I've successfully fed small freshwater fish to tarantulas.

evening in many parts of the country. Beetle larvae like mealworms are taken by some tarantula species.

Mammals

Many keepers feed small rats and mice to their tarantulas. Newly-born mice and rodents are often used, and they are referred to as pinkies. This prey type is messier than most others and the remains tend to decompose quickly. Some people have had success feeding frozen mice to their tarantulas. Live adult mice have been reported to injure tarantulas upon occasion.

Pinkie mice are a good supplement to a diet that usually consists of insects. They can be quite messy, though, so be prepared.

Prepared Foods

Until recently, spiders were thought to require live prey. These days, most spiders, tarantulas included, are classified as predators/scavengers. Small groups of tarantulas have been observed feeding on dead mammals on the sides of roads in South America and in Texas. Many tarantula species will find and accept beef heart and other meat. Basically, what you feed your tarantulas is what you have most easily available.

Feeding and Food Problems

Despite many rumors to the contrary, it's probably not possible to overfeed a tarantula. There are many reasons why keepers supply seemingly excessive amounts of food. A well-fed female tarantula with a very plump abdomen is bound to produce more eggs than a thin female.

A classic and frequently asked question concerning tarantulas is: Why won't they eat and what can be done about it? The period between feedings can be critical only for small tarantulas in their first few instars. Young tarantulas can be weakened if not fed every few days, depending on the species.

Tropical fish flakes are popular and inexpensive foods that can be used to increase the nutritive value of crickets prior to being offered to your spiders.

Dealers have withheld food deliberately before shipping early instars because there's less chance of the spiderling molting in transit. A weak but hungry spider is thought more likely to survive shipping than a molting spider. Tarantulas should not be transported for at least a week prior to or after a molt because their exoskeleton will be soft and vulnerable.

Given appropriate prey, refusing to feed is not often a problem with younger spiders. The adults and larger immature specimens are a different matter. Seasons can affect hunger. Many North American tarantula species go for months without food during the colder parts of the year. In captivity at higher temperatures, withholding food might overly stress them. Larger tarantulas will not feed for days, weeks, or even several months before a molt. This is normal and only a water dish is needed. Some species seem to be champions at not eating. Three adult female desert blond tarantulas *(Aphonopelma chalcodes)* refused all prey, drinking only water for well over 3 years.

Another feeding problem is called shipping syndrome. Wild caught tarantulas that are severely dehydrated (or perhaps starved) when shipped from their native countries may look healthy, but are unable to eat even though they can catch prey. They deteriorate over weeks or months until they finally die.

Food and Feeding

After 3 or 4 months without food, and with no indication of an impending molt, some action should be taken. Change is the key. Raising the temperature is the first step, and the most successful. Some say to raise humidity, although this can cause lots of other problems. People preferring a winter temperature of around 68°F and summer temperature of 78°F or so should find ways to heat their tarantulas cages. For most tarantulas, a minimum temperature of 75°F with a maximum of somewhere in the mid to upper 80s will work.

Varying the diet may also get a stubborn tarantula to eat. Try different prey items. I've had many tarantula individuals ignore some prey species, but immediately attack others.

One last consideration about prey items is the relative strength of the prey. Some tarantula keepers have used large, powerful dung beetles as prey, and the tarantulas were injured or killed by the dung beetles. Don't feed anything to your tarantula that may be able to overpower it.

Spiderlings

Feeding live prey to very young and tiny tarantulas can be a problem since finding appropriately-sized prey (pinhead crickets or *Drosophila* flies) can be difficult for many keepers. Early instars of many tarantula species will readily accept adult crickets or other insects that have been killed and split in half or cut into pieces. You may not notice they are eating the split insects since the bodies don't seem to get any smaller, but most if not all spiderlings will eat using this method.

Selected Species
of Tarantulas

Many people still buy their tarantulas from pet shops, although the Internet is quickly becoming a more popular outlet for tarantula keepers. Pet stores are often highly limited in the species selection that they offer and they may not be able to tell you exactly what species they are selling, nor anything about how to successfully keep them, unless they have an employee who is well-versed in tarantula identification.

Below are some of the most common tarantula species found in pet stores and on the Internet. The scientific name is listed first. Many of the more advanced hobbyists only use scientific names while novices tend to prefer common names. The common names below are only official in the United States and Canada. Outside of that region, only Australia has a standardized list of arthropod common names.

Aphonopelma anax / Texas tan tarantula (United States, Mexico)

The known range stretches from Kingsville, Texas, south to the Rio Grande River and most likely into Mexico. It is usually found not far from the Gulf Coast, and how far west or north it may range from there remains unknown. The urticating hair is the airborne type, but it's not very noticeable or irritating to most people. Females may live more than 20 years. Most males rarely live more than 2 months after maturing. However, occasionally a male may survive a year and a half or more in captivity. In nature, the life span of the male, once it abandons its burrow in search of females, is likely measured in minutes, hours, days, or at most weeks. This also applies to the males of most burrowing species.

Texas tan tarantulas are a popular species in the United States, well known for being easy to care for and nondefensive. Since many Aphonopelma species are similar looking, several other species are sold under the name of Texas tan tarantulas; the mistake—or deception—is apparently not often noticed. Many people may wonder why their Texas tan tarantula never reaches the larger size the species is supposed to reach. The most likely explanation is that they never had a Texas tan tarantula in the first place.

These are one of the few tarantula species known that have benefited from the presence of man. In the southern parts of Texas, they can be found in large numbers on domestic grass lawns and mowed lots. In natural areas, you may have to search for days to find a burrow. In the lawns of many of the small towns of southern Texas, you may find a burrow a meter in any direction. They seem to prefer mowed lawns under or near mesquite trees more than anywhere else.

Aphonopelma bicoloratum / Mexican bloodleg tarantula (Mexico)

This species is from central Mexico. Since it's officially illegal to export wildlife from Mexico, we may never know where it's from. The urticating hair is airborne. Females may live 20 years or more.

This species is one where color patterns can be used to identify the species with a good degree of confidence. The abdomen is brown with a smattering of red hairs. The carapace is red, as are the patella, tibia, and metatarsus of the legs. Mexican bloodleg tarantulas are almost certainly burrowers, and should be treated as such. Since we don't know if the species came from deserts or tropical forests, the standard operating guidelines are to supply dry substrate with a retreat and a water dish. Keep a close eye on the spider to see if it spends a disproportionate amount of time hanging over its water dish.

Aphonopelma chalcodes / desert blond tarantula (United States, Mexico)

This burrowing species is adapted to the deserts of southern Arizona and northwestern Mexico. The carapace and chelicerae are covered with a golden tan hair that is

often shining. The abdomen is brown with some reddish hair, and the legs are also brown with a bronze hue. The overall form of the spider's body can be a good identifying character for those familiar with North American *Aphonopelma*. The urticating hair is airborne, but is not known to cause significant irritation in most people. Females may live 20 or more years.

Some believe this species is a classic obligate burrower, but in captivity, it may not choose to burrow even if given the chance.

This species is infamous for long periods of fasting, chronically worrying many keepers. They tend to show little defensive behavior.

Selected Species of Tarantulas

Aphonopelma moderatum /
Rio Grande gold tarantula
(United States, Mexico)

Some think that *Aphonopelma moderatum* is the most striking of all United States tarantula species. They range from around Del Rio, Texas, south along the Rio Grande River to at least Rio Grande City. They are likely present on the other side of the river in Mexico. The abdomen is brown with golden hair. The carapace is brown, as are the legs, which sport golden and brown hair. Urticating hair is airborne, but is not known to cause much irritation. Females may live for 15 to 20 or more years.

Aphonopelma moderatum is a burrowing species, and many individuals tend to show a fairly high degree of defensive behavior when disturbed.

Aphonopelma seemanni /
Costa Rican zebra tarantula
(Central America)

The Costa Rican zebra tarantula hails from the forests of Costa Rica. Some claim it's also found in Nicaragua, El Salvador, and Honduras. This burrowing species is one of the most popular and frequently sold tarantulas in the United States. The species largely resides in dry tropical forests.

Aphonopelma seemanni is an overall blue-black in color. The most significant distinguishing mark is the double white longitudinal lines along the tops of the legs, turning into a single line on the metatarsus and tarsus. Its urticating hair is airborne, and the females may live for 10 to 15 or more years. Many individuals may be skittish.

This is a burrowing species. Since the species can be a fairly water sensitive, it is a candidate for adaptation to drier conditions, unless you decide to keep it under humid conditions. Spiderlings are particularly water sensitive.

Avicularia avicularia / pinktoe tarantula (South and Central America)

Pinktoe tarantula distribution is widespread in the northern half of South America, Mexico, Costa Rica, Bolivia, Tobago, and maybe other countries. It's also found in Trinidad and may be expanding its range. Most are black, and often have iridescent blue-green highlights on the carapace and undersides of the legs. The tips of the tarsus of the legs and pedipalps are pink, hence the name pinktoe. The species has nonairborne urticating hair. Females may live from 4 to 10 or more years. This species exhibits little defensive behavior, and since it's an arboreal tarantula, it can survive being dropped many feet, making it a wise choice as a pet for children.

In nature, pinktoe tarantulas build tubular retreats on the trunks of trees and between leaves. Many build their retreats on houses, usually under the eaves of the roof. Adults generally prefer trunks. The immatures prefer leaves. They remain in the retreat during the day, coming out to hunt at night. They usually don't venture far from the retreat, but sit and wait for prey to come along. In one study, prey often consumed by pinktoe tarantulas included a good percentage of small geckoes.

Avicularia versicolor / Antilles pinktoe tarantula (Caribbean Islands)

As small immature specimens, Antilles pinktoe tarantulas are black with distinctive bright electric blue markings. As they grow, the coloration changes drastically several times until the adults appear either metallic blue or blue-green with orange abdomen and leg setae. This arboreal species have nonairborne urticating hair. The species is found on Martinique and Guadeloupe Islands in the Antilles Island chain. Females probably live up to 10 or more years. Most individuals don't often show much defensive behavior.

Selected Species of Tarantulas

Brachypelma albopilosum / curlyhair tarantula (Central America)

Curlyhair tarantulas are reported to be found in large numbers in Honduras, Costa Rica, and Nicaragua in the seasonal tropical forests. The species is similar to Brachypelma vagans. The cephalothorax is dark brown with tan hair on the margins. The abdomen is brown to black with numerous long, slightly wavy, tan hairs with a touch of orange. The legs are colored much as the abdomen with the orange more pronounced on the metatarsus. Airborne urticating hair is present, but is not much of an irritant to most people. Females may live 10 to 15 or perhaps 20 or more years.

This is a burrowing species. This species is rather tolerant of moister substrate conditions and may prefer them. Young spiders should be kept on moist substrate with higher humidity; they will often burrow readily. Defensive behavior is usually absent in curlyhair tarantulas, but you can always end up with a skittish one.

Brachypelma auratum / Mexican flameknee tarantula (Mexico)

This species was previously suspected of being a highland form of Brachypelma smithi in Mexico. Because these animals are worth so much in the pet trade, the true location of many species is basically kept secret by profit-motivated collectors. The legs and abdomen are black with a red flame shape on the dorsal part of the patella. A white horizontal stripe appears at the joint below the flame shape. Upon first seeing one, it appears as if somebody painted a flame pattern on the patella of some other Brachypelma species. The carapace is very similar to B. smithi; black with tan or whitish areas around its edges. The urticating hair is of the airborne variety, but hasn't been reported as more than mildly irritating by keepers. A degree of defensive behavior is found only rarely in some individuals. Females may survive 15 to 20 years or longer. Mexican flameknee tarantulas along with *B. smithi* individuals are for sale in some Mexican cities. In Reynosa, a Mexican city across the Rio Grande River from the city of Mission in southern Texas, adult females of these two species are sold for about $20 to $25. Unfortunately, a jail term could be waiting for you if you're caught bringing them back into the United States

Brachypelma boehmei / Mexican fireleg tarantula (Mexico)

Another close relative of *Brachypelma smithi*, the Mexican fireleg tarantula is a burrower found in Mexico. It can be separated from other species in the *B. smithi* group by coloration. The carapace is black with orange hairs, and the abdomen is also black as is the femur on the legs. The chelicerae have a tinge of red. The patella, tibia, and metatarsus of the legs are a bright red/orange. The urticating hair is airborne, and as with the other *Brachypelma*, is not known to be especially irritating. The species does not show much defensive behavior, but many consider it more skittish than others in the genus, and some may be downright maniac hair kickers. Female lifespan is suspected to be 15 to 20 or more years.

Brachypelma emilia / Mexican redleg tarantula (Mexico)

The Mexican redleg tarantula is found in Mexico. The black triangle marking on the carapace is a good indicator to separate it from other *Brachypelma* species. The abdomen is black; the tibia and metatarsus of the legs are a red/orange color, and the rest of the leg segments are black. This is one of the most sought-after species in the United

States and Europe. The urticating hair is airborne, but is not noted as much of a problem. Females may live 15 to 20 or more years, and in one case, a female was thought to be in excess of 35 years of age.

Brachypelma emilia is a burrowing species. Most show little defensive behavior, but some are jumpy.

Brachypelma smithi / Mexican redknee tarantula (Mexico)

Overall, this burrower is dark brown to black, with pale orange longer setae on the abdomen and legs. The carapace has a distinctly shaped *B. smithi* color pattern of a black center, with a light pattern around the edges. The term redknee is used because the patella is red or orange, unlike the species most confused with it, *Brachypelma emilia*, in which the patella is dark. Female life expectancy runs up to 20 or more years.

The urticating hair is airborne. Most people don't react to it, but some do. This species is popular and common in captivity, and is often nondefensive, leading many to handle them, but some are real hair kickers, especially when younger. Some enthusiasts lose their sensitivity to the hair after a number of contacts. Others may become more sensitive to the hair over time. Still others continue to react to the hair about the same way as they initially did. This applies to all types of urticating hair..

Brachypelma vegans / Mexican redrump tarantula (Mexico, Belize)

The Mexican redrump tarantula is a wide-ranging species in central and southern Mexico. It is also in Belize. Some allege the species can be found in Costa Rica and Colombia, but offer no evidence to support the claim. The species is black with the femur a deeper black color. The abdomen has red, orange, or brown setae. These hairs are also evident on the tibia and metatarsus of the legs. The urticating hair is airborne, but it is not particularly aggravating to most people. Female life expectancy is the *Brachypelma* standard of 15 to 20 or more years. Many consider the behavior of the Mexican redrump tarantula a tad toward the touchy side.

Someone in Florida released *B. vagans* there (whether accidentally or on purpose) and a small number of them were able to survive in a localized area in or near a citrus orchard. Some are still there despite the state's agriculture department attempts to eradicate the harmless and beneficial animal. *Brachypelma vagans* is a burrowing species.

Chromatopelma cyaneopubescens / greenbottle blue tarantula (Venezuela)

This colorful species is popular. The carapace has a metallic green/blue sheen and the abdomen is dark with orange setae in adults, striped in spiderlings. The  legs are mostly covered with deep blue hair. The urticating hair is airborne, but is not known as being unusually irritating. However, there are always individuals more sensitive than others to the hair. If the female lifespan is known, it hasn't been widely reported. A lifespan of ten to15 or more years is likely for the females of the species.

This is a burrowing species, at least as adults. Immature *C. cyaneopubescens* are thought to not burrow in their natural habitat of dryer grass and shrub land. They make a convoluted web reminiscent of some arboreal tarantulas around the base of grasses and shrubs. Later, as adults, they are thought to excavate burrows in the soil. In captivity, they spin copious amount of webbing, making cage height a little less problematic.

It was at first thought that the species needed higher moisture levels, since they were from South America, but experienced keepers report a damp environment can injure or kill them quickly. Spiderlings, however, require higher moisture levels. Defensive behavior tends to be on the light side.

Some individuals apparently can grow to adulthood in just over a year. Developmental time is temperature dependent. As with nearly all tarantula species, there are some quirky individuals that won't grow quickly, no matter how high the temperature or how much they are fed.

Citharischius crawshayi / king baboon tarantula (Africa)

Found largely in Kenya, this species is one of the most popular of the African tarantulas. The overall body color is a shiny reddish brown to orange with red setae. *Citharischius crawshayi* is thought to be on average the third or fourth largest tarantula from Africa. The species has no known urticating hair. Individuals may readily use stridulating organs when disturbed. The stridulating organs consist of modified stiff setae, which they rub together, mostly on the chelicerae. Since captive bred specimens are common but usually slow to reach adulthood in captivity, most females continue to be wild caught. Females probably live 10 or more years. Many individuals are highly defensive with little provocation.

Citharischius crawshayi dig deep burrows often at the base of acacia bushes. Cage height is very important, especially with these large, heavy burrowing species. The immature specimens are notorious for erratic feeding habits and slow growth.

Cyclosternum fasciatum / Costa Rican tigerrump tarantula (Costa Rica)

The carapace of this burrowing tarantula has a copper orange colored hair. Their range is central Mexico to Costa Rica. The setae on the legs and abdomen have a peach hue. The tiger stripe patterning on the otherwise black abdomen is orange or copper, but may be reddish in some individuals. This is a distinctive and popular tarantula species. Urticating hair is present and airborne. Behavior may be described as touchy. Female lifespans may go 10 to 15 years or more.

Grammostola rosea / Chilean rose tarantula (Chile)

This species has undergone a number of scientific name changes, a process that may not yet be completed. Some years ago, *Grammostola cala* was popularly thought of as the Chilean rose tarantula, while *Grammostola*

spatulata had the name the Chilean common tarantula. Red individuals were considered *G. cala*, while brown individuals were thought to be *G. spatulata*. When both red and brown forms were reported emerging from the same eggsac, workers began checking into it. They found *G. cala* was rare or not in the pet trade; it is from a different region of Chile and looks different than *G. spatulata*, which is thought by some to be coming into the trade in two color morphs (one browner, one more pinkish-frosted in appearance) from different areas of Chile. *Grammostola cala* was removed from the AAS common names list, since a species has to be common enough to warrant a name; the Chilean rose tarantula common name was given to *G. spatulata*, since that species was already being sold so frequently as the Chilean rose tarantula. Later, *G. rosea* was found to be the same species as *G. spatulata*. Since *G. rosea* was described first, it became the senior synonym and that name was retained.

Through all these changes, the scientific name changed, but the common name remained the same. Large numbers of adults and large immatures are collected and shipped to the United States and Europe. They are probably the tarantula species most frequently sold in pet stores.

Some individuals are a dark brown to brownish red with pinkish setae, others more toward brown with some red setae, and some with a brown, often bronze look. Urticating hair is present and airborne, but is not particularly irritating compared to some species. A female's lifespan can reach 10 or 15 to 20 or more years. Most individuals exhibit little defensive behavior, but there are a few recalcitrant individuals.

Selected Species of Tarantulas

Haplopelma lividum / Cobalt blue tarantula (Asia)

Although in the pet trade for some time now, *Haplopelma lividum* was not described until 1996 from specimens out of Myanmar (Burma) and Thailand. The abdomen is black with some gray and a bluish sheen, often with a chevron pattern. The carapace is blackish gray with a hint of blue. The chelicerae are grayish blue, and the clypeus above the chelicerae is pink. The legs are various shades of blue, ranging from dull blue to iridescent blue. This species has no urticating hair, and most individuals are quick to the defense. Females probably live up to 10 or more years.

This species is a burrowing one and is probably an obligate burrower in nature. It was once thought that they needed to be kept almost wet to survive. It's now known they can be gradually adapted over to dry conditions if they are given lots of attention during the process.

Hysterocrates gigas / Cameroon red tarantula (Africa)

This species hails from Cameroon in western Africa. The species is deep brown with red setae. Some of the setae on the legs are grayish red. Individuals of this species are frequently sold to the unsuspecting as *Hysterocrates hercules*, a species that probably exists, but is apparently not collected in significant numbers. No urticating hair is known in the species. Females probably live up to 10 years or more.

The species is a burrower from savannah grasslands of Cameroon, while some claim they're found in tropical rainforests. It's possible they are found in both places, since Cameroon ranges from tropical rainforests in the south to savannas in the north. They are thought to be highly defensive.

Quick & Easy Tarantula Care

What makes this species so admired over many others is the behavior of the spiderlings and smaller immature specimens. Spiderling from the same eggsac can be kept together communally up to 6 months or more before cannibalism occurs. As many as 200 spiderlings can be kept in a sweater box-sized cage, which must be escape-proof as the spiderlings are active at night and can easily slip out past a loose lid.

Feeding the spiderlings consists of killing adult crickets or other insects and tossing them into the cage. The spiderlings emerge and group feed, usually five or more individuals to one cricket simultaneously. On one occasion, I saw a small group of spiderlings feeding on every available space on a cricket. I rolled it over and there was another spiderling feeding on the cricket upside down. They can be entertaining to watch, but be sure to supply them well with food. After they get to a certain size, cannibalism will occur.

Lasiodora parahybana / Brazilian salmon tarantula (Brazil)

This species can get huge, coming close to or occasionally getting larger than some of the other giants, such as *Theraphosa blondi* and *Theraphosa apophysis*. Unlike many *Theraphosa*, they rarely lose abdominal hair and remain quite handsome between molts. The carapace is deep brown with a hint of red and salmon hair around the edges. The abdomen is black with salmon setae. The legs are brown with salmon setae, and the chelicerae are a brownish black. Urticating hair is present and airborne. Some hobbyists have reported urticating hair in this species is much more irritating to the skin than that of most tarantula species. Others haven't had that problem. Females may live 10 to 15 or more years. They are generally slow to show defensive behavior.

A large burrowing species from the Brazilian rainforests, cage height is a most important consideration. The large, soft abdomen need not fall far to rupture, which kills the animal quickly.

Selected Species of Tarantulas

Psalmopoeus cambridgei / Trinidad chevron tarantula (Trinidad)

The coloration in this species is subtle. The carapace is brown with a greenish tinge and a light brown rim around the edges. The dorsal abdomen is flesh colored, with a distinct dark chevron pattern. The legs have orange zig-zag stripes on the metatarsus, and a black spot on the tarsus leading into an orange spot further toward the claws. Many have more green overall. Two longitudinal orange stripes are on the patella and go down part way onto the tibia. The species is said to lack urticating hair despite its new world origins. Females may live up to 10 years or more. Most are defensive when disturbed.

This is an arboreal species, and because most web up the cage profusely, many keepers leave the cage floor bare.

Pterinochilus murinus / Mombassa golden starburst tarantula (Africa)

Found originally in Kenya, this species is allegedly in Zambia and Tanzania. It is one of a potentially large number of color morphs that used to be grouped under the name "Usambara" followed by some color or another.

The abdomen and legs of one color morph of P. murinus are a yellow brown with a hint of gray and green, and the long setae are a subdued yellow. The legs have white hair at the joints. The black carapace sports a golden starburst pattern radiating out from the center. Urticating hair is not known from this species. Females may live 5 years or more. There are at least two other color morphs including red and orange. This species is highly defensive for little or no reason, probably more than any other commonly kept tarantula species.

Although this species webs profusely, it should be treated as a burrower. This is one of the toughest tarantulas that exist, seemingly thriving on neglect.

Quick & Easy Tarantula Care